HOW TO GROW A CHILD

HOW TO GROW A CHILD

* * *

A Child's Advice to Parents

Bernard Percy

Ann Arthur, Linden Jackson, Lori Johnson,
Crystal Kornegay, Beth Wallace, Reggie Wright

ACTION
PUBLISHING

C O N

With thanks and admiration for my wife and daughters, the great joys of my life; with appreciation and friendship to Ann, Lori and Linden, I so greatly value our relationship; and a special thanks and tribute to Tom Solari—you shared in the vision for this book for over thirty years, your friendship, support and inspiration are truly admired and appreciated.

ISBN 13: 978-1-888045-24-6

Library of Congress Control Number: 2009938909

Manufactured in the United State of America
10 9 8 7 6 5 4 3 2 1

Action Publishing LLC, PO Box 391, Glendale, CA 91209
Visit us online at **actionpublishing.com**

T E N T S

1

YOUR EXPECTATIONS MAKE THE DREAM COME TRUE

"Where much is expected of an individual he may rise to the level of events to make the dream come true." —ELBERT HUBBARD

There is an often-told account of a middle school teacher in Minnesota who had a remarkable year with her students. They achieved wonderful results on their academic tests, and, perhaps more importantly, were enthusiastically involved in their studies, completing high-level, truly challenging projects and activities.

The principal went to the teacher at the end of the school year to congratulate her and commented, "This is the best job of teaching I have ever seen. What your students accomplished is something very special. I am very proud of what you have done."

The teacher modestly responded, "Thank you, but it wasn't very difficult. After all these were very gifted students, with very high IQs." The principal was surprised by her comment. He knew that this was really an average academic group of students, not known for their high IQs or special talents and he asked, "What do you mean?"

The teacher pulled out a slip of paper from her desk with her students' names on it and said, "Here are their IQ scores." The principal looked at the paper and saw: John—165. Diana—159, etc. He put the paper down, looked at the teacher in amazement and said, "These are not their IQ scores, these are their locker numbers."

This teacher's expectations had been so high that she created

Barnard's daughter, Dhyana, age 5, making her dreams come true.

challenging projects, and demanded a standard of performance and achievement from herself, as well as her class, that she "knew" could be attained. It was truly *her* expectations that were the foundation of the success of her students. How do you think the students would have performed had their locker numbers been in the range of 90 to 110, and the teacher thought they were below average in their intellect and capability?

Are YOU underestimating the true potential of your own children because of what others have told you, how you were raised, or the limited expectations of educators and others who influence their lives?

As Ann Arthur, one of the authors of *How to Grow a Child* wrote when she was eleven years old, "How can a child believe in herself when no one believes in her."

It is a biological fact that if you place goldfish in a small bowl, no matter how well you feed them, they will only grow to a very small size. If you take the same fish and put them in a pond or larger body of water they will grow to a much larger size. How big is the pond you are creating in which your children will grow? How are you helping your children believe in themselves and rise to the level of events to make their dreams come true?

Your child's confidence in themselves and what they might accomplish (the size of the pond) is strengthened by having a trusted parent who listens to them and values their viewpoints. Read and "listen" to the voices of the children in this book; they speak the truth we need to hear.

Most importantly, discover the voice of your children.

While children seem to expect a "saintly" level of perfection from their parents, the secret of meeting those expectations is not "perfection" but what the children wrote in *How to Grow a Child*. After you read this book, do the surveys in the last chapter with your children and be ready to evaluate what you are doing (or not doing). May what you discover help you be the "saint" your children expect you to be, so they can be who they are!

What do you think?

*   *   *

Bernard Percy with his 1974 5th grade class at PS289 in Brooklyn, NY. Lori Johnson (front left) is one of the authors of *How to Grow a Child*. "I always wanted my classes to know when to call me 'Bernie' and when it was 'Mr. Percy.' Clearly, this was a 'Bernie' moment."

THE STORY OF HOW TO GROW A CHILD

"A teacher affects eternity; he can never tell where his influence stops." —HENRY BROOKS ADAMS

On a September day in 1974 I was looking forward to starting my tenth year as an elementary school teacher at Public School 289 in Brooklyn, New York—alive with the anticipation and excitement of the possibilities, the dreams and plans I had for the new year and all the great things that I could do for my students. My favorite moment was when the students filed into my class for the first time. The knowledge that I would be responsible for the quality of their lives over the next 10 months was a challenge that I truly relished.

As I stood by my 1964 Volvo 122S, happily welcoming the students as they eagerly arrived for their first day of school, I saw Ann Arthur walking toward me.

Ann Arthur, 10-year-old author and inspiration for this book.

Ann had been in my 4th grade class, a wonderful child and a bright, hardworking and dedicated student; the kind of student who makes you love being a teacher. "Hi Mr. Percy, I want to show you something I have been working on this summer. I think it's about time adults heard from children how to raise children, not just other adults, and I have been working on a manuscript. Can I show it to you?"

She handed me her manuscript and I sat down on the fender of my car, very interested in what she had written. One of the first lines that I read was, "Look into your child and you shall see your reflection."

The impact on me of that simple truth was very powerful and I immediately turned to Ann and said, "Ann, this book should be published, and if you want, I will help you do that."

That moment changed my life, as it has changed the lives of the children who wrote this book.

With Ann's agreement I put together a workshop with Ann and five other students who had previously been in my classes. I selected students, ages 10 to 14, who I knew could uniquely communicate their thoughts and represent the voices of other children their age. I invited all the students to my house for a special workshop and made them an offer.

I explained what an "advance" was (a payment one gets to write a book before the book is written) and offered each of them a $10 advance. I gave them the option to retain their status as amateur writers and refuse the advance. Needless to say they all became professionals that day.

Their book was indeed published in 1978. Their thoughts, viewpoints, understandings and advice have influenced so many others throughout the years. And they listened to their own advice as they grew up and raised their own children.

What is especially gratifying to me is that my continuing relationship with Lori, Ann and Linden has resulted in this new edition of the original book.

Ann, the originator of the book concept, is now the mother

The student authors—from left: Lori Johnson, Linden Jackson, Ann Arthur, Reggie Wright, Crystal Kornegay, Beth Wallace—photographed in New York four years after writing *How to Grow a Child*. The first edition had just been published. Bernard Percy's friendship with Lori, Linden and Ann has remained close for over thirty-five years.

Linden, then and now. "I'm proud of who my son is becoming. I've lived by my principles, and he has picked up on them as well."

of two children and a pediatric ophthalmologist. Her thoughts resonate with the special quality of our enduring friendship, "I am amazed that I still have a relationship with my 4th grade teacher. Knowing Bernard is a life-changing experience. I wanted my voice understood as a child; Bernard acknowledged and valued what I had to communicate. His love and respect for me (and for children in general) is what I carried with me over the last three decades."

Likewise, Ann's legacy has helped me better understand and know what I really wanted to achieve, and helped me start on that road to achievement. From teacher to author (seven books on parenting and education) to editor, and editor in chief, the wisdom of these young writers has enriched every aspect of my life.

Teachers do affect eternity, but so do students!

Linden, the father of one child, has among other things written a comprehensive, almost scholarly, work on the music industry and the history of music—an amazing accomplishment.

His sense of adventure and willingness to overcome numerous obstacles has truly been an inspiration to me all these years.

I still remember how Linden rode miles through the streets of Brooklyn on a bike with no brakes, holding in one hand his mom's bread pudding, which he knew I loved, braking the bike by pressing his foot on the front tire, trying to find the exact street where I lived (having only been there before by car or train).

"I was very excited when my former 5th grade teacher, friend and life mentor Bernard Percy first asked me to help with the *How to Grow A Child* book. What I wrote back then still holds true, my thoughts and feelings have remained the same—don't think that kids are stupid. Coming to the U.S. as a Jamaican, I had to fit into the Black community, and then into the White community that I was exposed to. What I gained from that experience were thorough lessons in RESPECT, VISION, and WISDOM. My son has certainly picked up where I left off, as he is popular with all races at his school and neighborhood. I'm proud of who he is becoming. I've lived by my principles, and he has picked up on them as well. My son will keep his values, and will hopefully pass them on to his kids, too."

Linden has been my friend, and yes, mentor, over these years as well.

Lori, a professional communicator extraordinaire, also became the parent of two daughters and a son. The advice that she and her fellow authors offered now influences her own children.

"As I look back over the thoughts I expressed in *How to Grow a Child*, I can't help but feel especially proud that as a parent, I adhered

Lori with her three children. "...as a parent, I adhered to the things I felt
most strongly about."

Ann with her two children. "Of all the things I have done thus far (medical school included), parenting/mothering has been the most humbling."

to the things that I felt the most strongly about. My overriding theme seemed to be respect. The times we live in are by far different than the 70s but I believe the basics still remain the same." She added, "It is really profound to still be in touch with my 5th grade teacher who is still concerned about what I think and feel, and know that these are valued by him. Being in his class is the most memorable and most real of any class I have ever been in."

Who has influenced whom the most? Lori's sincerity, genuine care and values have motivated me and helped to define the values that I most appreciate in others.

As parents or teachers, as in all human relationships, when we can see and acknowledge the importance of other people and their viewpoints—especially those of our children—wonderful things become possible, even as the next generation takes on the challenges of parenthood.

Ann said, "Of all the things I have done thus far (medical school included), parenting/mothering has been the most humbling of experiences. In *How to Grow a Child*, I wrote 'Vacation is when your child is grown.' That line haunts me. I see my children, particularly the oldest, Camille, as 'clay'—to be molded and formed by her father and myself. As a parent, you are entrusted with this little seedling of a person. I know I will make mistakes. What haunts me is that I will never get the opportunity to do it all over again. I really believe my children would agree that as they grew, I respected them as the little people they were."

It has been 30 years since the book was first published. The common sense wisdom and practical advice written by the students is as applicable today as it was then. And if there is a sort of magic at the heart of their story, I think it is this: The ideas and beliefs originated by these children took life when they were valued and acknowledged by others. That is a magic that every parent can create by respecting and valuing the unique ideas and viewpoints of their children.

Bernard with wife, Caralyn, and their three daughters.

I couldn't have anticipated, on the first day of school in September of 1974, that these children would bring a change to my life that would help me fulfill my life's dreams and ambitions. I have raised my own children—three wonderful daughters—and work daily to help parents and kids improve and enrich their relationships. And I am still friends with Ann, Lori and Linden—although they still insist on addressing me as "Mr. Percy." Over the years I have tried to locate Reggie, Beth and Crystal, the three other writers, but have not been able to find them.

Ann's reflections are the perfect way to send the book forward to new generations of parents and children The content and clarity of her writing truly reflect who she is and why this book has such enduring value.

Revisiting How to Grow A Child
by Ann Arthur

It has been more than thirty years since I first began my journey into the wonderful world of writing. *How To Grow A Child* was born out of my desire to communicate my thoughts, feelings and insights. I was ten years old when I approached Mr. Percy with a copy of my manuscript. In 1974, my Brooklyn was a gritty, rhythmic, exciting and somewhat frightening place. School and writing became a refuge for me.

My parents were West Indian immigrants struggling to raise

seven children. They had a strong work ethic but little money. They ruled with an iron fist. Children were seen and never heard. We were the post–civil rights babies with a real chance of "making it" in America. (That is if we respected adults, never questioned authority and ate all our veggies!) It was expected we would stay in school and become accomplished adults but there was little room to be a bright, outspoken, confident child.

While nothing could have fully prepared me for the adventure of parenting, when I read the pages of *How to Grow a Child*, I am moved to reflect on several key elements.

One, the assertion, by children, that their feelings, voices, emotions COUNT.

I am a child and I know how a child feels.

We're just as much people as our parents.

Two, these child-writers clearly know something about the importance of nurturing children.

It takes a great amount of responsibility, love and patience.

It's not really fair to have a child knowing you'll not have time to spend with him, and not be able to teach, love, help, support and care for the child properly.

Three, these child-writers manage to celebrate the innocence of their youth without losing sight of the goal of becoming wonderful, independent adults in their own right.

If parents could become children again for a little while, I think they could be a better judge of their children's problems.

Parents must be able to show their child the right path to the stem of a good life.

In the almost three decades since the publication of *How To Grow A Child*, I have been blessed with the opportunity to attend college, medical school and create a new family of my own. However, I count as one of the seminal events of my life meeting Bernard Percy, being his student and participating in the creation of *How to Grow a Child*. It's where I got my wings and everything—every dream I had—seemed to fall into place. I went from being a shy girl to a confident "sista"—comfortable in her own skin.

Bernard Percy's love and respect for me (and for children in general) is what I carried with me over the last three decades. I took it with me to Brown University as an undergraduate and to the Yale University School of Medicine. I embrace it today as I practice Pediatric Ophthalmology in my hometown of Brooklyn, New York. I emulate it in my daily struggle to be a great parent and role model for my own children.

I am proud of this new edition, proud of the children who wrote it and proud of the friendship with our teacher Mr. Percy, which allowed this dream to come true. Thirty years later, *How to Grow a Child* still offers inspiration, encouragement and hope for parents and the children they love.

Ann Arthur-Andrew,
Brooklyn, New York

*　　*　　*

What follows are the orignal voices of Ann, Lori, Linden, Reggie, Beth and Crystal as first published in 1974 (below). Listen and learn, as I have, and then have a chat with your children. They have much more to tell you. —Bernard Percy

HOW TO GROW A CHILD

* * *

A Child's Advice to Parents

Ann Arthur, Linden Jackson, Lori Johnson,
Crystal Kornegay, Beth Wallace, Reggie Wright

Look into your child
and you shall see
your reflection.

Ann

**Kids are people.
I don't see why that's
hard to understand.
We have faults,
we have problems.
OUR BIGGEST
PROBLEM IS
GROWING UP.**

Reggie

*What is the purpose of
being a parent?*

*A very hard question
indeed.*

*But if you don't know
the answer,*

*With children you'll
never succeed.*

*Didn't you even think
that maybe
a child would know?*

*To tell you the truth,
I didn't think so!*

Beth

VACATION IS WHEN YOUR CHILD IS GROWN

It takes a great amount of responsibility, love and patience. It takes an awareness. It's an all-day, all-night job; "VACATION" IS WHEN YOUR CHILD IS GROWN.

Ann

A Child's Beginning Soil

Drop in large amounts of love, sprinkle on encouragement and understanding from your heart above. Shower with patience, but do not spoil, and now you have a perfect child's beginning soil. *Ann*

It's not really fair
to have a child knowing
you'll not have time
to spend with him, and not
be able to teach, love, help,
support and care for
the child properly.

Linden

If a parent and child can't
get along with one another, then
they shouldn't be together.

Crystal

Make your relationship with your family a memorable one, for there is no second chance.

Ann

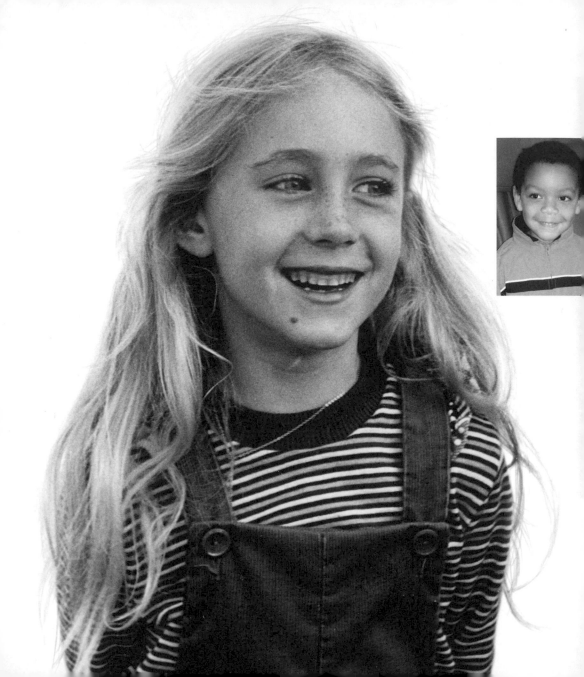

A Child Speaks

Teach me to know how to be on my own,
But do not send me into the world alone,
Love me truly with all your heart,
For I pray our relationship will not fall apart.
Listen to what I have to say,
Do correct me when I'm wrong, if you may.
Direct me to the path of happiness, so my life
   will be truly wonderful, and nothing less.
Educate me to respect myself and others,
   I beg of you.
Therefore I can be respected too.
Guide me to speak only the truth,
And maybe one day, I'll be an almost
   perfect youth.

Ann

KIDS ARE PEOPLE TOO

Children should be treated equally as adults. I'm not talking about household jobs, but respect.

Ann

Children
are people
and they should
be treated as people.
Children have feelings...
We want respect too.
If adults expect us to
respect them, then
respect us too.
After all, we
are people.

Lori

*Many people
look down on kids and
it's not because we're
short either.*

Beth

*We're just as much
people
as our parents.*

Crystal

Some people think children are bouncing balls; do this, do that, and a lot of other things. Kids are people and should be treated that way. You were children once, too, so why don't you treat them the same way you would've liked to be treated.

Crystal

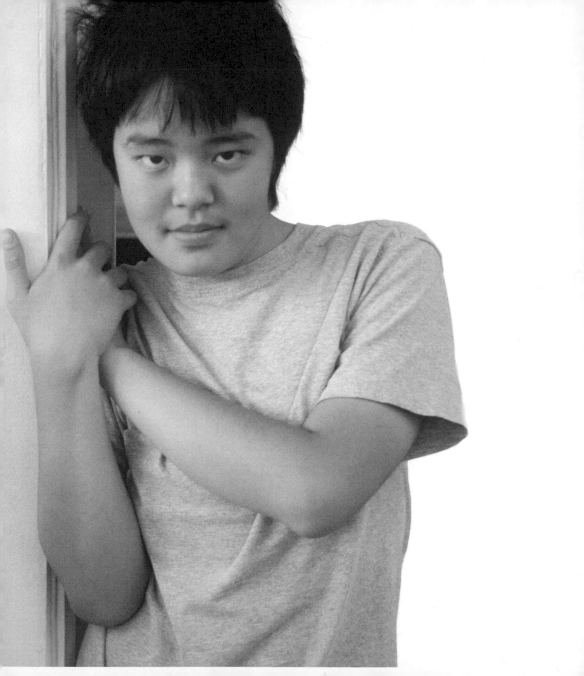

I'm a person
not a *toy*.
I feel what
you feel,
Maybe even
more.

Ann

OH MY LORD, FOR GOODNESS' SAKE, I WON'T LET YOU MAKE THIS MISTAKE.

Oh my Lord, for goodness' sake,
I won't let you make this mistake.
I did the same thing when I was a child,
Then I cried for a week and my mom went wild.
Please don't do this and don't do that,
Cause you'll get hurt, and that's a fact.

Reggie

If you always tell children what to do, they'll depend on you or someone else for the rest of their lives.

Beth

A child has to learn to be
independent.
Prepare your child to stand
on her own two feet.
Parents won't always be
with their child to show her
right from wrong.
A child has to learn to
make decisions.

Ann

Let children decide things for themselves.
For example, if it's raining outside the parent
shouldn't say, "It's raining outside,
wear your raincoat!" The parent should say,
"It's raining outside and maybe you
should wear your raincoat."
Of course your child won't agree with you
all the time and think she should
wear (or do) something else. Even if you
know the child is wrong,
let her make her mistake; it's the way
she's gonna learn.

Linden

Joys of Parenthood

Now since you're twelve I think you should
know the joys of parenthood.
It isn't always fun and games,
picking out clothes or choosing names.
It's more than telling a beddy bye tale
or buying bootees at a Macy's sale.
Patience and love are the key
to mastering this great responsibility.
You see in the parenthood game of give and take,
even the best tend to make a mistake.
But even when you seem to fall,
you must rise to the occasion and answer the call.
So keep your cool and at all cost
never tell your child to get lost.
Because...if they sink beneath you or rise above,
the thing they'll remember is your unmistakable love.

Reggie

Children learn from experience,
They ought to learn life.

Crystal

I ACT OUT THE ACTIONS I SEE

When you know
you are wrong, admit it.
Don't be ashamed because
you're the head of your child.

Lori

**Some parents just can't
accept the idea that they made
a mistake in growing up
their child.**

Linden

Listen my parents and you shall hear
The voice of your child,
That sweet little dear.
Mom, Dad, you're an example of what I'm to be,
For I act out the actions I see.

Ann

Manners are a thing that must be learned
as far as Mom and Dad are concerned.
They teach us to say "Thank you,"
"You're welcome" and "Please,"
and not to say, "Gimme those peas."
Manners of parents and children are the same,
but the way some parents act,
is really a shame.
You want us to be perfect and that's a fact.
But when we go out, you don't know how to act!

Reggie

CHILDREN DON'T APPEAL TO NOISE OR SLAPS

Dig yourself, beat on my head,
Dig yourself, my clothes are all red.
I see beating, if I do something wrong,
But every night it's the same old song.
First with a mop handle,
then with a broom,
And before I know it,
Pow! Bang! Zoom!
And if you get me on the floor,
You don't stop, you want more.
JUST BECAUSE YOU HAD A BAD DAY
YOU TAKE IT OUT ON ME
IN EVERY WAY.
This isn't punishment, this is cruel,
And if you want my opinion,
it just ain't cool!

Reggie

Parents should teach with respect.
Not to hit 'em because they didn't eat their
Wheaties,
Or something dumb like that.

Lori

Screaming and slapping usually don't work,
Because kids get so upset and confused when
they're being shouted at,
Screamed at, or hit, that they forget what you
are trying to tell them;
They get so mad about being hit or shouted at,
they don't care about the reason
for the violent action.
Children don't appeal to noise or slaps.

Ann

Many parents beat
their children,
And not in races.

Crystal

Some of the time
punishment is given
not to make the
child do better,
but to give the parent
a feeling of security.
I think it's wrong
to make a child do
something unpleasant
so the parent can
feel good.

Reggie

Don't take back a punishment

from your child...

If you tend to let your child

"off the hook,"

He'll continuously get into

trouble.

Ann

"Johnny" thinks his
punishment is really
severe.
Now he thinks his parents
don't really care.
He says, "Why can't I
help you punish me?"
Now he's happy 'cause
he punished himself,
You see?

Linden

PARENTS FORGET WHAT HAPPENED TO THEM WHEN THEY WERE CHILDREN

PARENTS FORGET
WHAT HAPPENED
TO THEM WHEN
THEY WERE
CHILDREN; how their
emotions were, and the
way certain situations
came up as children and
what they did about it.
If parents could become
children again for a little
while, I think they could
be a better judge of their
children's problems.

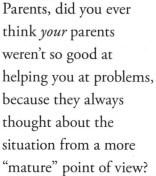

Parents, did you ever
think *your* parents
weren't so good at
helping you at problems,
because they always
thought about the
situation from a more
"mature" point of view?

Beth

Put yourself in a position
which your child is in.
If they get beat up, pretend you did too;
If they have a chance to go away,
Pretend you do too, etc.
By doing this it will come clear to you
how they feel.
You can switch places
for a while with
your children.
They can become
the parents and
you the children.
Not only may your
children realize
how hard the parents' job is,
But it may open your eyes too.
This will help you both get along better.

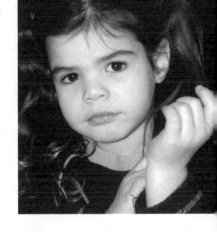

Crystal

Parents must be like a tree:
They must have branches
Like open arms that welcome all
their children.
A bark able to stand rain
like tears and problems,
storms and
arguments.
Roots making a
tree stand on its
own and nourish
itself,
like the route
you need to guide
your child to independence.
Like leaves, you must explain
to your child,
the changes he will go about
during his life.
Parents must be able
to show their child the right path to
the stem of a good life.

Ann

IF YOU CAN'T TAKE MY VIEW STAY OUT OF MY LIFE

*How can a child believe in herself
when no one believes in her?*

Ann

Parents should not embarrass their child, they should not call them stupid, bighead, skinny, or other names that might embarrass them in front of their child's friends or in public. Some parents discuss their child's faults in front of relatives and friends. Why bring out your private business in the open? Do you want to embarress or punish your child? When parents (or children) are without manners, they make their personality look very childish and silly.

Ann

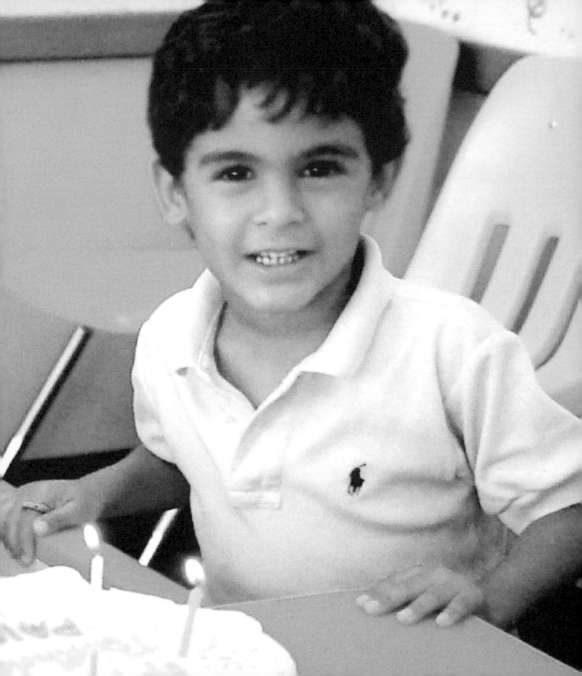

Without
encouragement,
they may just be dead
inside.

Crystal

You need not agree with the child's point of view

t children should have a say in any matter. Ann

**Don't correct or embarrass kids in front of other people.
It messes up pride.**

Linden

Children don't
understand things
the way adults do;
They tend not to be
as complicated as adults;
They see things for
what it's worth now,
not ten years
from now.

Reggie

I listen to everything you say,
Just like a sap,
But when I have an idea,
you rap.
I always, I mean always
listen to you,
But you don't care about my
point of view.
You decide how my life
will be run,
Like you are the ruler
under the sun.
When I try to help
with the master plan,
You put my ideas
in the garbage can.
Remember it's my pain,
my joy, my strife,
So if you can't take my view,
stay out of my life.

Reggie

WE'LL TALK ABOUT IT TOMORROW

When you communicate with a child you'll have a happier life.
Your child should be your closest friend...
Communicate as both a friend and a parent.
If you wouldn't say something to a friend, don't say it to a child.
Isn't she your friend?

Beth

Some parents make promises

that they can't keep.

The parent ends up not

keeping the promise

and the child loses confidence

in the parent...

This will eventually make a

barrier between the child

and the parent.

Linden

...if your child finds out you lied, he'll probably not believe you next time.

Reggie

*Kids nowadays have
different talk and signs.
Learn the new ways and
you'll be alright...
Listen to the things they say,
talk about and how they
react to the things you say.
How about making a family
hour and you can discover
how they feel about things.*

Crystal

Children sometimes

feel so relaxed,

That they can really

express their thoughts

with adults.

Ann

If you have a problem
That you cannot get an answer to,
Ask your son or daughter,
Maybe they can give you a clue.

Crystal

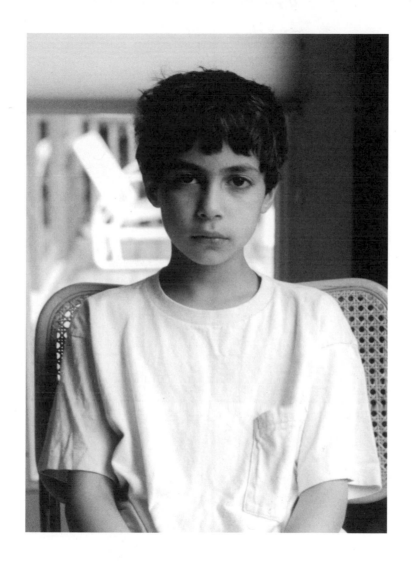

If you have a problem ask
your child about it.
Their answer may or
may not help,
But it lets your child
know that you know
they're alive.

Crystal

**Talking to your child
isn't enough.
You've got to play
around
And do a lot of stuff.
You may say that
this is silly,
the whole block knows
I love my "Billy."
Check this out and you'll see
that I'm right,
if you don't communicate,
Your child will turn you
off
...like a light.**

Reggie

*You can communicate with
children not only by talking,
Because I think action
speaks louder than words.
All talk is very nice,
but when you are needed,
Are you there?
Think about it.*

Reggie

*I used to ask my mother things and she told me
to go ask my father.
I would ask him and he sent me to my mother.
I never did get the answers, .
But I did get....dizzy.*

Linden

Some parents don't talk
to their children.
Do we have body odor?

Beth

**If you shut off a child completely,
Sooner or later she's going to break wild
and do something you'll be sorry about.**

Lori

*A child can't grow up thinking
what he has to say doesn't count.*

Ann

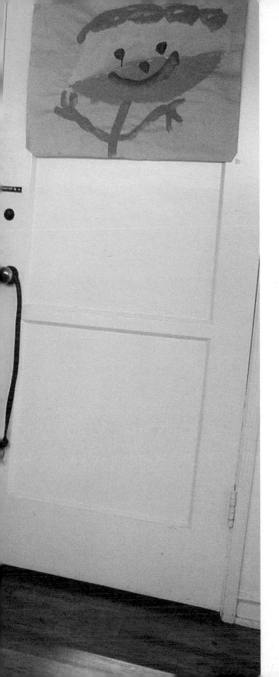

Many parents say to their children,
"We'll talk about it tomorrow."
What is tomorrow?
Another day to say,
"We'll talk about it tomorrow."

Beth

What is a Child?

A child is a person full of many
    wonders and ideas.
A child can express and reason in
    family discussions and decisions.
A child is a person worthy of the
    warmth of love and affection.
A child should be taken seriously,
    respecting his desires and dislikes.
A child is a person who shouldn't
    be pushed in a direction that
    he doesn't think he would enjoy or be happy.
A child is a person who learns
    from the surroundings he lives in,
And those surroundings should be
    of love, trust and understanding.

Lori

I am a child and I know

how a child feels. *Ann*

IMPROVING YOUR RELATIONSHIPS

"The key question to answer is, "How well are you really doing growing your child—from your point of view and theirs?"—BERNARD PERCY

When I consult with parents and children, I often use these relationship evaluation questionnaires. Their purpose is to help parents attain greater awareness and understanding of their child's viewpoint—as well as the child better understanding the parent's viewpoint when the child and parent share answers. The responses to the evaluations become a foundation for enhancing or improving their relationship.

For example, at one workshop a stepfather and his stepson, who did not get along well, each answered the evaluation questions. At one point the 12-year-old boy began to cry. His stepfather asked him what was happening, and the boy said, "I really don't know how to answer the questions about what you love to do [in Part 2 of the Evaluation form 2]. I was never interested enough in you to know more about you." The stepfather then began to cry, and that moment drew them closer together than they had ever been, and it greatly changed their relationship for the better.

Evaluation form 1, "Survey 1", is based on the points of view stressed by the youngsters who wrote this book. There is no scoring or attempt to judge who is the "better" parent. All that is asked is that you be objective when considering the questions and then be as honest as possible with yourself as you seek to learn from your responses.

Evaluation form 2, "Survey 2," is in three parts. It is a way of determining how well you and your children know and understand each other.

It is recommended that you have your child do the evaluations with you. Answer the questions separately from your children (helping them to understand the questions where needed) and then compare answers. In the case of younger children, you can ask them for their answer after you have completed the evaluation. As *How to Grow a*

Child has already demonstrated, your children's viewpoint can lead to new insights, and improve the quality of your relationship, no matter how good it is already.

As you go over the results of the evaluation, be willing to hear what your children truly think. Do not try to persuade them to have a different point of view, or that they don't understand you, or any number of ways that you can set up an "I am right, you are wrong" mentality and battlefield of words. Be willing to see things from their point of view and find out what is right about what they are communicating. Find those points you can honestly agree with after really hearing and understanding their point of view. Let them know you do understand what they think or believe, and even let them know where you honestly feel they are right and you are wrong.

Once you have done that, then work with your children to find agreements that you both align with and will keep.

EVALUATING YOURSELF

This survey is written for parents based on the points stressed by the children in How to Grow a Child. *After considering their answers, parents may also ask their children to answer the same questions. Compare responses and you should be rewarded with some wonderful revelations.*

1. Do you spend "enough" time with your child?
2. Do you get along with your child?
3. Do you treat your child as "people"?
4. Do you respect your child?
5. Do you show your respect for your child?
6. Do you allow your child to make his/her own mistakes and learn from those mistakes?
7. Do you allow your child to decide things for him/herself?
8. Are you there for your child when needed?
9. Do you always tell your child what to do?

10. Do you "practice what you preach"?

11. Do you admit your mistakes to your child?

12. Do you punish your child to help the child do better or to give you a feeling of security?

13. Do you punish your children in a way that will upset and confuse them, so that they won't care about the reason for the punishment?

14. Do you let your child "off the hook"?

15. If you had a bad day, do you take it out on your child?

16. Can you see things from your child's point of view?

17. Do you allow your child to have a say in any matter?

18. Does your child know that what he/she has to say counts?

19. Do you embarrass your child in public or in private?

20. Is your child your close friend?

21. Do you really listen to your child?

22. Do you compliment and encourage your child? When? How often?

23. Do you believe in your child's rightness and abilities?

24. Do you believe in the rights of your child?

HOW WELL DO YOU KNOW EACH OTHER?

The surveys are written for parents and children to do together: How well do you know and understand each other? Answer the questions separately and then compare and discuss your answers.

Part 1

1. What do your children/parents most like about you?
2. What do you most like about your children/parents?
3. What do you do together that is most fun and enjoyable?
4. What can you do to make your children/parents laugh?

Part 2

1. What are three things your children/parents love to do?
2. What are the three most fun things you do *with* your children/parents?

3. What things do your children/parents like to do by themselves; with friends?
4. What things do you like to do by yourself; with friends?
5. What would you most like to change about your children/parents?
6. What would your children/parents most like to change about you?
7. Can you see things from your children's/parents' point of view?

Part 3

1. Do your children/parents know that what they have to say is important to you?
   Never   rarely   sometimes   often   usually   always
2. Do you really listen to your children/parents?
   Never   rarely   sometimes   often   usually   always
3. Do your children/parents really listen to you?
   Never   rarely   sometimes   often   usually   always
4. Do you feel your children/parents are really interested in what you have to communicate?
   Never   rarely   sometimes   often   usually   always

EPILOGUE

*"Everything turns out alright in the end.
If it isn't right, it isn't the end."* —ANONYMOUS

Things will turn out right in the end with your willingness and ability to understand and value your child's point of view.

Ann wrote, "Look into your child and you shall see your reflection." Things will turn out right in the end when you evaluate your expectations and learn from the reflection you see as you look into your child.

I leave with one final quote found in the book,

Lori wrote, "A child is a person who learns from the surroundings he lives in, and those surroundings should be of love, trust and understanding."

Give your child that love, trust and understading, and may the very best be the very worst you know!

Bernard Percy

How to Grow a Child: A Child's Advice to Parents

This book was designed by Michael Manoogian and typeset by Lea Frechette. The text was set in Garamond, the headlines in Futura. The photo retouching was done by Allen Harris. Printed and bound by Thomson-Shore.

Photo Credits

Cover © Ann Arthur
3 © Bernard Percy
6 © Bernard Percy
8 © Bernard Percy
10 © Bernard Percy
12 © Linden Jackson
15 © Lori Johnson
16 © Ann Arthur
18 © Frank Ofman
24 © Michael Manoogian
26 © Cam Solari
27 © Cam Solari
30 © Michael Manoogian
30 © Michael Manoogian
31 © Michael Manoogian
32 © Carl Smith
35 © Michael Mannogian
36 © Edgar Metzler
37 © Edgar Metzler
38 © Cam Solari
38 © Cheryl L. Duncan
39 © Brenda Shahinian
39 © Sampsa Koskenalho
39 © Michael MacGregor
39 © Luciano Apperti
42 © Michael Manoogian
43 © Carl Smith
44 © Caralyn Percy
45 © Arpin Manoogian
46 © Michael Manoogian
50 © Cam Solari

52 © Caralyn Percy
54 © Michael Manoogian
57 © Scott Menaul
59 © Edgar Metzler
60 © Michael Manoogian
61 © Osnat Plaut
64 © Michael Manoogian
65 © Michael Manoogian
66 © Cam Solari
68 © Cam Solari
72 © Michael Manoogian
74 © Michael Manoogian
75 © Edgar Metzler
77 © Cam Solari
78 © Brenda Shahinian
79 © Michael Manoogian
82 © Brenda Shahinian
82 © Jessica K. Workman
82 © Roy Deschene
83 © Shelly Hussey
83 © Michael Manoogian
84 © Michael Manoogian
85 © Osnat Plaut
86 © Cam Solari
87 © Antranig Shahinian
91 © Michael Manoogian
92 © Scott Menaul
93 © Luciano Apperti
93 © Jessica K. Workman
93 © Linda Pedrazzini Shahinian
94 © Russi DeVitre

96 © Cam Solari
97 © Cam Solari
99 © Cam Solari
100 © Jessica K. Workman
102 © Michael Manoogian
103 © Michael Manoogian
106 © Michael Manoogian
107 © Keri Topjian
108 © Shelly Hussey
109 © Brenda Shahinian
110 © Michael Manoogian
110 © Michael Manoogian
111 © Michael Manoogian
112 © Osnat Plaut
112 © Scott Menaul
112 © Edgar Metzler
112 © Brenda Shahinian
112 © Osnat Plaut
113 © Sharon Shahinian
115 © Brenda Shahinian
116 © Shelly Hussey
117 © Michael MacGregor
118 © Michael Manoogian
118 © Michael Manoogian
118 © Michael Manoogian
121 © Pat King
122 © Michael Manoogian
124 © Carl Smith
127 © Cam Solari
129 © Bernard Percy

Add your child's advice...